Specialist Fourth Class
John Joseph DeFazio

BY THE SAME AUTHORS

Julia C. Davis
Empowering English Language Learners (contributing author)
Keeping the Dream Alive: A Reflection on the Art of Harriet Lorence Nesbitt (contributing author)

Jeanne C. DeFazio
Creative Ways to Build Christian Community (editor with John P. Lathrop)
How to Have an Attitude of Gratitude on the Night Shift (with Teresa Flowers)
Redeeming the Screens (editor with William David Spencer)
Berkeley Street Theatre: How Improvisation and Street Theater Emerged as Christian Outreach to the Culture of the Time (editor)
Empowering English Language Learners (editor with William David Spencer)
Keeping the Dream Alive: A Reflection on the Art of Harriet Lorence Nesbitt (author)

Bruce I. McDaniel
Lost Persona (author)
The Hardest Part: Homecoming Stories from the Vietnam War (author)
Walk Through the Valley: The Spiritual Journey of a Vietnam War Medic (author)
Walk Together Earth Mother Children (author)

Martha Reyes
Keeping the Dream Alive: A Reflection on the Art of Harriet Lorence Nesbitt (contributing author)
Redeeming the Screens (contributing author)
Jesús y la Mujer Herida (*Jesus and the Wounded Woman*) (author)
Jesucristo, Tu Psicólogo Personal (*Jesus Is Your Own Personal Psychologist*) (author)
Por Que No Soy Feliz (*Why Am I Not Happy?*) (author)
Quiero Hijos Sanos (*I Want Wholesome Children*) (author)

Specialist Fourth Class John Joseph DeFazio

Advocating for the Disabled American Veterans

JOHN JOSEPH DEFAZIO

Edited by
Jeanne C. DeFazio

Foreword by
Julia C. Davis and Martha Reyes

Afterword by
Bruce I. McDaniel

RESOURCE *Publications* • Eugene, Oregon

SPECIALIST FOURTH CLASS JOHN JOSEPH DEFAZIO
Advocating for the Disabled American Veterans

Copyright © 2020 Jeanne C. Defazio. All rights reserved. Except for brief quotations in critical publications or reviews, no part of this book may be reproduced in any manner without prior written permission from the publisher. Write: Permissions, Wipf and Stock Publishers, 199 W. 8th Ave., Suite 3, Eugene, OR 97401.

Resource Publications
An Imprint of Wipf and Stock Publishers
199 W. 8th Ave., Suite 3
Eugene, OR 97401

www.wipfandstock.com

PAPERBACK ISBN: 978-1-5326-9883-5
HARDCOVER ISBN: 978-1-5326-9884-2
EBOOK ISBN: 978-1-5326-9885-9

Manufactured in the U.S.A.   JANUARY 6, 2020

This book is dedicated to my uncle William DeFazio, a United States Army Staff Sergeant who was disabled in World War II's Battle of the Bulge, and to my uncle Andrew Fernandez, who served in the Pacific in the United States Navy during World War II.

—John Joseph DeFazio

Contents

Foreword I | ix
  Julia C. Davis
Foreword II | xiii
  Foreword by Martha Reyes
Preface | xix
Acknowledgements | xxi

Advocating for Disabled American Veterans | 1
  John Joseph DeFazio

Afterword | 13
  Bruce I. McDaniel
About the Authors | 22
Bibliography | 25

Foreword I

JULIA C. DAVIS

THREE OF MY BROTHERS served in the United States military. Solomon Butler served in the United States Army and the United States Marines. Quincey Butler served in the United States Navy in the Pacific and then in the Naval Reserve. Franklin Butler served in the United States Air Force in Vietnam. His service-related injuries are physical due to exposure to Agent Orange and psychological due to a Post-Traumatic Stress Disorder from combat. Franklin's disability rating is 85 percent.

I thank God daily for Franklin's disability rating, which gives him a decent standard of living and quality healthcare. According to the Harris Federal Employees Law Firm article "Veterans' Affairs (VA) Disability Benefits";

> Disability-specific benefits have been available to U.S. soldiers since the time of the American

Foreword I

Revolution. The veterans' disability system, however, has never been perfect. Of the 217,000 people who served in the American Revolution, only 3,000 ever received benefits. Among WWI veterans, 85 percent of all disability claims were denied. Today, 31 percent of claims are denied—and 60 percent of those denials are in error.[1]

As an African American author and educator, I am concerned about the high ratio of homeless veterans who are African American. The National Coalition for Homeless Veterans "Background and Statistics" included these facts from the United States Department of Veterans Affairs (VA):

> Roughly 45% of all homeless veterans are African American or Hispanic, despite only accounting for 10.4% and 3.4% of the U.S. veteran population, respectively.[2]

The United States Department of Housing and Urban Development's 2018 "Annual Homeless Assessment Report to Congress" explains:

> African Americans comprise one-third of veterans experiencing homelessness but less than one-quarter of veterans experiencing unsheltered homelessness (24%). While African Americans comprise a smaller share of veterans experiencing homelessness than of all people experiencing homelessness, they are overrepresented as compared to their share of all U.S. veterans (12%).[3]

---

1. Harris Federal Employees Law Firm, "Veterans' Affairs (VA) Disability Benefits," lines 1–5.

2. National Coalition for Homeless Veterans, "Background & Statistics," lines 8–9.

3. U.S. Department of Housing and Urban Development, "2018

Foreword

I reside in the Boston area. On February 13, 2019 at 9:55 a.m., Bob Ward at Boston 25 News reported that John DeGraff, a U.S. Navy veteran, has been living in a tent in the middle of downtown Boston for eleven years.[4] I am glad to see that the Disabled and Limbless Veterans are helping John get assistance from the Veterans Administration. It hurts my heart to see disabled veterans homeless on the street. I pray for them and give what I can. They deserve the care and support they need. I am engaging in this dialogue to advocate for equality in disability ratings for all veterans but emphatically for disabled veterans of color.

Contact me. If I can help you, I will.

Telephone: 781-393-4517
Email: jdavis.ema@gmail.com

Annual Homeless Assessment Report," 54.

4. Ward, "Homeless Vet Living in the Shadows."

Foreword II

Martha Reyes

My uncle Sergeant Pedro Luis Gomez and my cousin Sergeant Esteban Mendoza served in Vietnam and were exposed to Agent Orange in combat. My family did not lose these loved ones on the battlefield but both died after a long battle with cancer brought on by exposure to chemical warfare. I thank God daily for their disability rating, which gave them quality care and the dignity of shelter on their journey home to heaven. I am participating in this dialogue as a Californian and as a Hispanic author and psychologist to gain support for the increasing population of Californian and Hispanic homeless veterans.

The statistics are alarming. The webpage "Homeless Veterans in the United States" reports:

> As of January 2017, the state of California had the highest number of veterans experiencing

homelessness. There were an estimated 11,472 homeless veterans.[1]

The Department of Housing and Urban Development, in its "2018 Annual Homeless Assessment Report to Congress," explains:

> Just under 19 percent of all individuals experiencing homelessness identify as Hispanic or Latino. The share of individuals identifying as Hispanic varies by sheltered status, accounting for 15 percent of the sheltered population and 23 percent of the unsheltered population.[2]

Current research identifies a high percentage of California's disabled veterans suffer from service-related mental illness and self-medicate with drugs and opioids and end up with legal problems.

Jude Litzenberger, executive director of the California Veterans Legal Task Force, identifies a common dilemma of disabled American veterans:

> Service members or veterans with PTSD, traumatic brain injury, military sexual trauma, substance use, or other mental health conditions caused by their military service get DUI misdemeanors because they self-medicated instead of seeking mental health treatment.

The California government allocates funds annually for the care of disabled veterans, but many of them are unable to follow through on the process of claiming the financial support that is available. California State Senator Hannah Beth Jackson details California Senate Bill 725,

---

1. "Homeless Veterans in the United States," lines 41–45.
2. U.S. Department of Housing and Urban Development, "2018 Annual Homeless Assessment Report," 22.

signed by Governor Jerry Brown in 2017, to help these veterans and to protect public safety:

> This bill clarified once and for all that these veterans are eligible for pretrial diversion programs, it will also ensure that veterans and service members who have served our country will get the help they need to address substance abuse and mental health issues.[3]

I was glad to learn that Riverside County, California is housing disabled and homeless veterans in its Housing First Program. KPBS's reporter, Amita Sharma, in her May 18, 2018 report, "The only city in California to solve veteran homelessness is on a mission to go bigger," cited the testimony of Riverside resident Bill Bruick, a former homeless veteran whose depression and alcoholism had hobbled him since leaving the Army in 1996:

> Army veteran Bill Bruick spent his last night homeless lying on a tiny patch of dirt, now festooned with a pink flowering shrub behind a Food 4 Less grocery store in Riverside. There were no bushes, Bruick said, pointing to the exact spot still remembering the lump in the ground. I slept right here. I liked it because nobody could really see me back here. Nobody ever parked back here. I got lucky you know. That night in 2013 capped 10 years of living outside a shopping center for the 51-year-old Bruick . . .[4]

Because of Riverside's Housing First Program,[5] Bruick was able to get off the street and now works to place homeless veterans in city housing.

---

3. "Governor Jackson Signs Bill," lines 14–16, 19–22.
4. Sharma, "Only city in California," lines 4–8.
5. Housing First, https://www.riversideca.gov/homelesssolutions/

I empathize with the millions of United States veterans who struggle financially. My father died unexpectedly in my childhood and I experienced financial hardship.

The United States Veterans Affairs report entitled "Veteran Poverty Trends" explains:

> The poverty rate for Veterans ages 18–34 years old is higher than those between the ages of 35–54 years old. The poverty rate for Veterans ages 55–64 years old are higher than those of ages 65 and over.[6]

Breaking a cycle of poverty is a challenge. Katherine Gallagher Robbins and Anusha Ravi, in their report published by the Center for American Progress entitled "Veterans Living Paycheck to Paycheck Are under Threat during Budget Debates," explain:

> Analysis by the Center for American Progress reveals that 3.9 million veterans, more than 1 in 5, are living paycheck to paycheck at 200 percent of or less than the federal poverty level. Thirty-seven percent of Native American veterans, 30 percent of African American veterans, and 26 percent of Latino veterans are living paycheck to paycheck.[7]

Post-Traumatic Stress Disorder contributes to the challenge of survival for the disabled veteran. The Veterans Administration's disability claim process is often too complex and arduous a bureaucratic process for the mentally challenged disabled vet. Attorney Anne Lincott, in an entry

---

housing-first.

6. U.S. Veterans Affairs, "Veteran Poverty Trends," 5–6.

7. Robbins and Ravi, "Veterans Living Paycheck to Paycheck Are," lines 12–15, 18–21.

on her blog entitled "PTSD and Vietnam Veterans: Part Two: Substance Abuse," explains:

> The Vietnam War was an especially violent one and a high number of veterans were placed in combat situations. Today, this would seem like an obvious trigger for high rates of PTSD; however, following the Vietnam War, both the medical community and the general public didn't even think PTSD existed . . . Addiction and alcoholism often co-occur among veterans with PTSD. Because of the high rate of PTSD in Vietnam veterans specifically, addiction and alcoholism can also pose a significant problem for those that fought in Vietnam.[8]

The stresses of the current economy challenge us all. How can we help those who served in the military and have service-related physical or psychological disabilities? We can encourage them to get the help they need by driving them to a VA hospital or the Veterans Administration office. We can help them fill out forms. We can pray with them if they are willing to pray. If not, we can pray for them.

If you are a disabled veteran, contact me. If I can help you, I will.

Email: Dr.MarthaReyes@aol.com

---

8. Lincott, "PTSD and Vietnam Veterans," lines 6–9, 45–48.

Preface

DESPITE EVERYTHING I HAVE gone through as a disabled veteran, I am grateful for the opportunity to serve my country. The experience made me a better person. During my term of service, I was stationed north of Frankfurt, Germany at the Ayers Kaserne Kirch-Gons and served in the 2/36 Inf. of the 3rd Armored Division as a driver for Battalion S-3 and S-4 staff officers. I also served as a fuel and ammunition clerk in Germany for the battalion staff. While stationed in Fort Lewis, Washington, I served as a Scout/Forward Observer for Headquarters Company 3/47th of the Ninth Infantry Division. My military experience taught me to be alert. I recall walking by a cigarette thrown in the street in Ayers Kaserne/The Rock. The battalion Sergeant Major on post noticed this oversight and ordered me to pick it up and do twenty pushups. To this day, I don't litter. On the serious side, I suffered a service-related back injury in those years of service and today receive 100 percent disability.[1] In 2010–2015 I was employed by

---

1. "A service-connected disability is one that was a result of a

Preface

the United States Department of the Interior. I was forced into early retirement because my disability worsened. Ted Puntillo, Solano County's Veterans Service Officer, helped me get benefits.

I researched the status of the disabled American veterans and found that 4.3 million veterans, or 20 percent of all veterans, suffer from a service-related injury.[2] My loss of mobility put me in touch with other disabled veterans and made me realize the truth in Mother Teresa's statement, "If we have no peace, it is because we have forgotten that we belong to each other."[3] I am engaging in this narrative to gain support for all disabled vets, but emphatically for those with no legs in wheelchairs begging on the side of the freeway, those lying in the street self-medicating with alcohol, and those repeatedly incarcerated for drug use. These familiar figures risked their lives to protect the United States of America. I am here to stand up for them even if I have to use a cane, leg brace, and wheelchair for support.

—John Joseph DeFazio

---

disease or injury incurred or aggravated during active military service. Severity of one's disability is scaled from 0.0 to 100.0 percent, and eligibility for compensation depends on one's rating." U.S. Census Bureau, "Veterans Day 2017," lines 74–77.

2. U.S. Bureau of Labor Statistics, "43.3 Percent of Veterans," line 2.

3. Quoted from Brainy Quotes, https://www.brainyquote.com/quotes/mother_teresa_107032.

Acknowledgements

Thank you to Dr. William David Spencer for reading the manuscript and writing an endorsement. I am grateful for the help of my loving and thoughtful sister Jeanne, who was kind enough to assist me in putting my thoughts on paper. My cousin Louise Maguire, MSW, kindly encouraged me to apply for disability benefits. My wonderful friend Jeff McKillop has been a great inspiration. My niece Ella Louise Ryan is a bright light shining for all of us. The Mary L. Stephens Davis Branch Library helped greatly with the formatting of this book. My special thanks to Caleb Loring III and former United States Lieutenant Peter Lynch, who served in South Korea in the Second Infantry Division. Remembering every soldier who gave their lives in service.

—John Joseph DeFazio

Advocating for Disabled American Veterans

John, in Revelation 12:7–12, describes the last great angelic battle and Satan's ultimate expulsion from heaven.

> Satan, in his great pride and delusion that he can be like God, will lead a final rebellion against God. It will be a cosmic mismatch. Thus the dragon and his demons will lose the battle and be thrown out of heaven forever.[1]

Jesus' strategy for victory in the great war of heaven inspired me to write this testimony.

> Then I heard a loud voice in heaven say: "Now have come the salvation and the power and the kingdom of our God, and the authority of his Messiah. For the accuser of our brothers and sisters, who accuses them before our God day and night, has been hurled down. They triumphed over him (Satan) by the blood of the Lamb and

---

1. Got Questions Ministries, "Is the War in Heaven," lines 6–10.

> by the word of their testimony; they did not love their lives so much as to shrink from death. (Rev 12:10–11, ESV)

I am writing this testimony to triumph over the disability and horrific loss of mobility that I experience every day. I have faith that what I communicate in this book Jesus will use to overcome woundedness in my life, and in every disabled veteran's life who reads this book, because we are connected by the depth of our shared experience.

The Wounded Warrior Project website identifies

> . . . more than 52,000 servicemen and women physically injured in recent military conflicts. 500,000 living with invisible wounds, from depression to post-traumatic stress disorder. 320,000 experiencing debilitating brain trauma.[2]

I am sharing my journey to inform, support, and care for all of us.

FILING A DISABILITY CLAIM

I cannot stress enough the importance of always keeping military service records and military discharge documents, especially the "DD Form 214," to satisfy healthcare eligibility regulations.[3] I am forever grateful that Ted Puntillo helped me through the process of filing for disability. I cannot emphasize enough that all fellow disabled military

---

2. Wounded Warrior Project, "Mission Statement," lines 8–9.

3. "The DD Form 214, Certificate of Release or Discharge from Active Duty, generally referred to as a "DD 214," is a document of the United States Department of Defense, issued upon a military service member's retirement, separation, or discharge from active duty in the Armed Forces of the United States." Wikipedia, "DD Form 214," lines 1–3.

veterans should get in touch with their county Military Veterans Service Officer and become members of the Disabled American Veterans (DAV). Upon becoming a lifetime DAV member, I was informed that the DAV will further assist you with representation before the Veterans Administration and the Board of Veteran's Appeals.

I am including this excerpt from Ted Puntillo's article "How to Disagree with a Veterans Administration Decision" to help disabled vets in the process of gaining a disability rating. It is a long, involved process and claims are often initially denied. It's so easy to become discouraged. Guidelines are helpful:

> If the Veterans Administration issues a decision that you disagree with, do you have any options? Every day, the VA issues thousands of decisions that affect Veteran healthcare services, Veteran compensation, Veteran education and training benefits, and Veteran burial benefits. When they issue these decisions, they are required to include VA Form 4107, "Your Rights to Appeal our Decision."
>
> If the VA denies a disability claim, your first step would be to appeal the decision. Additionally, if you disagree with the disability percentage rating, or you think there is an error regarding the effective date, or, if you disagree with any other aspect of the decision, you may appeal the decision. The appeal process can take time and involve a lot of paperwork. But in the long run, the time initially spent on the appeal could pay off.
>
> Here are the steps, in order, that make up the appeal process.
>
> 1. Notice of Disagreement (NOD), a written statement that you disagree with a

decision the VA made regarding your claim. When submitting an NOD, you must be specific about your disagreement. If decisions were made on multiple items, be clear about which item you are addressing. A NOD can be accepted only if a final decision was made, and must be filed within one year of the date of the final decision. If you have missed the filing deadline, you may file another claim for the same condition or request that your previous claim be re-opened with new and material evidence

2. Statement of Case (SOC), a summary of the evidence considered, actions taken, decisions made, and the laws governing the decision. A SOC must be done when a NOD is filed and denied or when new evidence is received. Once the first SOC is completed on an appeal, subsequent SOCs are considered Supplemental Statements of the Case (SSOC). An appeal may have several SSOCs.

3. Formal Appeal—An appeal must be formalized, or "perfected" using VA Form 9, Appeal to Board of Veterans Appeals. This form must be received no later than either one year from the date of the decision letter or 60 days after the date of the Statement of the Case.

4. Hearings (Optional)—Hearings are held at the VA Regional Office by a Hearing Officer (HO) and provide an opportunity for claimants to present evidence in person.

5. Board of Veterans' Appeals (BVA), located in Washington DC, is the highest

appellate body in VA. Although most decisions are made in Washington, BVA does have travel boards that come to local offices. However, appeals can take from 2 to 4 years (or more) to decide.

6. United States Court of Appeals for Veterans' Claims (CAVC)

Because the VA has to adhere to laws and regulations that spell out exactly what proof is needed to substantiate a claim, the appeal process can be very lengthy, complicated and stressful for Veterans. Therefore, it is very important that the original claim be fully developed, providing all supporting evidence and documents required by the VA. By crossing all of your t's and dotting all of your i's, you can increase your chances of success the first time around.[4]

Ted Puntillo guided me through the claim process. I received my first 20-percent disability rating in 2004. It took approximately eight months to process. In 2007, I applied for a 40-percent disability rating, which I received in a year. In 2010, I qualified for a 60-percent disability rating, which I received in 2011. In 2011, I became a lifetime member of the Disabled American Veterans (DAV). The DAV contacted me and offered to represent me with the rest of my claim. The DAV attorneys began representing me and by 2014 my disability rating increased to 80 percent, which I received in 2015. The DAV attorneys automatically filed a Notice of Disagreement and in 2016 I received a 90-percent disability rating. At that time I was referred to a law firm by the DAV and I received a 100-percent disability rating in 2019.

---

4. Puntillo, "How to Disagree," lines 1–49.

Specialist Fourth Class John Joseph DeFazio

VOLUNTEERING WITH LOCAL VETERANS ORGANIZATIONS

I want to encourage disabled veterans to volunteer while filing a VA claim. I volunteered with local military organizations during the claim process. This gave me the opportunity to network with other disabled veterans. I loved having friends that understood what I was going through! We shared stories that made us laugh while we helped other military service personnel and their families. We learned so much from each other by lending a hand and raised money to help other service organizations. Each summer, as a Legion member, I helped organize breakfasts at American Legion Post 440 in West Sacramento, California and American Legion Post 77 in Woodland, California and worked at the parking booth at the Yolo County Fair. Proceeds from this activity maintained the American Legion lodges and the Yolo County Veterans Coalition vans to transport veterans to their medical appointments.

One local volunteer organization that is doing extraordinary work is the Farmer Veteran Coalition (FVC):

> It is a national nonprofit non-governmental organization that mobilizes veterans to feed America and transitions them from military service to farming. The Farmer Veteran Coalition is headquartered in Davis, California and was founded by Michael O'Gorman so that veterans might serve their country in a new capacity, as providers of the nation's healthier food and fiber.[5]

---

5. Wikipedia, "Farmer Veteran Coalition," lines 2–5.

STAYING ACTIVE AND INVOLVED WITHIN THE COMMUNITY

I do not participate in the Farmers Veteran Coalition, I am, however, an avid, happy gardener. I grow vegetables on my deck and herbs and fruit trees in my yard, and (with the help of my friend Mike Taesali) apply a drip and soaker system to irrigate without using excess water. I share what I grow with others in the community. Gardening provides a way for me to use my talents to help others and it's fun. I also like to cook, using fresh produce from the garden. I bring meals to seniors, mainly my mom, Inez DeFazio, and my Aunt Jane, prepared from my garden vegetables.

Years ago, my mother cofounded the Yolo County Coalition Against Hunger, which years later was renamed Yolo Food Bank.[6] She drove around in the community in her old orange truck picking up surplus produce from local growers to distribute to those in need within the county. Her efforts influenced my life. I still attend Yolo Food Bank events in support. My cousin Matt DeFazio, a director of Brown Construction Company, recently constructed the new Yolo Food Bank food distribution and operations facility in Woodland, California. Executive director Michael Bisch has done a remarkable job of keeping the Yolo Food Bank in operation as it meets the nutritional needs of more than 23,000 Yolo County residents annually, who are making 55,000 food access visits per month. I attend the Yolo County Food Bank events to show support and to be around people who make a difference.

Getting out and being with other people is really important when you are disabled. My brother Tom takes me fishing on his boat in the Sacramento River to catch striped bass. My friend Jeff and I go shooting together at

6. Yolo County Food Bank, https://yolofoodbank.org.

the Yolo Sportsmen's Association range. I take my cane and wheelchair for support if I need to go a distance since my ability to walk is limited. I have a wheelchair that I use when necessary. The important thing is to remain as active and involved as possible. I see a chiropractor and acupuncturist regularly to manage pain, but positive exchanges with others keep me from focusing on the physical pain I endure and give me the opportunity to get outside of myself. I urge my fellow disabled vets to find new friends and enjoy life despite health limitations.

STAY LITERATE

Reading provides a whole new world for me to explore. I am a lifelong lover of American history. I love reading about military history and how the Founding Fathers enacted the Constitution and the Bill of Rights as a compromise between pro- and anti-Federalists among themselves. The topic fascinates me because this compromise between the pro- and anti-Federalists allowed the ratification of the Constitution of the United States to maintain separation of powers and guarantee individual rights. I studied about and visited the Antietam Battlefield in Maryland, where the bloodiest day in United States history occurred with the loss of 22,000 on September 17, 1862.

Despite my loss of mobility, I plan to visit New England's Patton Park and have my photo taken in front of General Patton's tank in South Hamilton, Massachusetts. I also want to view the plaque commemorating the first cotton mill in America, in Beverly, Massachusetts, visited by George Washington in 1789. I am going to salute those remembered on the Revolutionary War Monument at Lexington Commons' "The Battlefield of the Nation." I want to wheelchair around as much of the Minute Men National

Historic Park as I can. I plan to see the canon at Independence Park, in Beverly. As Arianna MacNeill, in her article "Group, city eyes upgrades at Independence Park" explains:

> It was off shore from the park that the schooner Hannah engaged in battle with British naval ship the Nautilus, the first naval battle of the Revolution, according to the Beverly Historical Society. Independence Park is also where Gen. John Glover read the Declaration of Independence on July 17, 1776.[7]

As a retired disabled veteran, I owe a debt of gratitude to those who served before me. I read everything I can find about the Battle of the Bulge and Elsinborn Ridge, where Uncle Bill was deployed with his unit during the Battle of the Bulge. He was in Alpha Company 1/9 Regiment of the 2nd Infantry Division. A German tank drove over a foxhole, burying my Uncle Bill for three days in the snow. He was reported missing in action but found by Belgian civilians and hospitalized. Uncle Bill suffered from debilitating frostbite and a shrapnel wound to his right foot as service-related injuries for the remainder of his life. He never discussed his experience. Knowing what he went through made me think more deeply about the disabilities of other soldiers. I wanted to understand those who were injured and unable to express their own pain. Reading about soldiers from the past has given me the opportunity to empathize with their experience in battle and on the home front after service.

By staying informed about the lives of previous American soldiers, I realize that I am fortunate to be a disabled veteran of this era. I benefit from medical advances. The World Wide Web puts me in touch with other veterans instantly. Instagram allows me to view photos of friends

---

7. MacNeill, "Group, city eyes upgrades," lines 7–11.

and relatives in the military automatically. Organizations like the Wounded Warrior Project and Paralyzed Veterans of America are available online. Their websites allow me to read about medical advances for disabled veterans and encouraging testimonies of soldiers who overcome terrible loss. At a click, I can donate to help someone specific in need. The mission statement of the Wounded Warrior Project explains moving on from woundedness:

> Every warrior has a next mission. We know that the transition to civilian life is a journey. And for every warrior, family member, and caregiver, that journey looks different. We are here for their first step, and each step that follows. Because we believe that every warrior should have a positive future to look forward to. There's always another goal to achieve, another mission to discover. We are their partner in that mission.[8]

HAVE FAITH

I grew up in a Roman Catholic family. My Italian father and Spanish mother baptized me as an infant and sent me to Catholic grammar school, middle school, and high school. Catholic education taught me that God loves me and created me to seek *him*, to *know him*, to *love him* with all my strength. As a young child, I recall seeing a picture of Jesus above the blackboard lovingly embracing children from every race and color. That image remained with me. To this day, I keep a painting of Jesus in my room to look up to and a Jerusalem Bible in my living room to read.

My faith in Jesus was tested in the military and as I suffered a service-related back injury and loss of mobility.

---

8. Wounded Warrior Project, "Mission Statement," lines 1–6.

I prayed to Jesus through the whole process. He understood my frustration and loved me. The love of Jesus kept me from despair, alcohol, and drug abuse. The Lord was on my side and I thanked him every day for sticking it out with me. I wouldn't be alive today without Jesus. I love him with all my heart and wrote this book to share his love with other disabled veterans. If you are out there feeling all alone as a disabled veteran, I want you to know that I love you, and most importantly, Jesus loves you and is right there for you. Ask him. He will come into your heart and support you. He will never let you down.

CONCLUSION

In this brief book I have shared my personal experience with the disability rating process and guidelines to process disability claims with the Veterans Administration. I have explained why volunteering with local veterans organizations is a good thing to do. I have mentioned how staying active and involved within the community is beneficial. I have also discussed why reading to stay informed is helpful. In the introduction, I quoted Revelation 12:10–11:

> Then I heard a loud voice in heaven say: "Now have come the salvation and the power and the kingdom of our God, and the authority of his Messiah. For the accuser of our brothers and sisters, who accuses them before our God day and night, has been hurled down. They triumphed over him [Satan] by the blood of the Lamb and by the word of their testimony; they did not love their lives so much as to shrink from death.

Disabled soldiers *did not love their lives so much as to shrink from death.* They risked their lives serving their

Specialist Fourth Class John Joseph DeFazio

country. We triumph in the spiritual battle by caring for them. If you can, please give generously to veterans organizations. If you can't give money, the next time you see a homeless veteran on the street, give a kind word or prayer and thank them for their service. If we all did this much, we would bring salvation and power and the kingdom of God, and triumph over Satan by the blood of the Lamb.

If I can help you, I will.
Email: jjdefazio@gmail.com

Afterword

Bruce I. McDaniel

Every veteran has a story. And every story deserves to be heard. Whether it is a story of combat or peacetime service, whether it focuses on time in the service or the effects after return to civilian life, every veteran's story is part of a greater whole. Every veteran's experience is unique. Besides the obvious differences in military branch and rank, within the military there are many different jobs.

On the day I enlisted in the Army I traveled with a bus full of new recruits to Fort Dix, New Jersey. In my hand I held my orders, listing thirteen other young men besides myself, along with the MOS (Military Occupational Specialty) for which each of us had enlisted. Even in that small group, eight jobs were represented: Wire Maintenance, Infantry, Motor Transit, U.S. Army Security Agency, Airborne/Unassigned, Engineer Heavy Equipment Operation and Maintenance, Clerical, and Medical Care and

Treatment.[1] Imagine, at the height of the Vietnam War, the different stories those jobs might have led us to!

Besides his or her specific job, the historical context affects a veteran's story. Was the country at war when he or she served? Did he or she serve in a theater of war, or in one of the many other places, at home and abroad, where the United States military is present? Was the general public supportive of the war and of military service? Was there opposition to the war, and was the veteran demoralized by stories of protests back home? Or was the country indifferent, civilian pursuits monopolizing attention while ongoing wars faded into the background? The experiences of people in the military will reflect each different period in our nation's history.

Each veteran's story is unique because veterans are unique people. What was the veteran's attitude toward serving at the time he or she entered the service? During the period when I served the draft was in effect; there was an expectation that boys would someday serve in one of the armed services. Many of the soldiers I served with had been drafted and showed no enthusiasm for the military or the war we were fighting. For those who enlist voluntarily, there are as many different motivations for serving as there are veterans: adventure, proving oneself, continuing a family tradition of service, to name a few. For some, patriotism plays a role, especially during times of national crisis. An example from my time would be the anti-communism prevalent during the height of the Cold War; we all knew President Kennedy's words, "Ask not what your country can do for you—ask what you can do for your country."[2] A more

---

1. McDaniel, *Walk Through the Valley*, 11. The author's experiences serving in the Army and coming home to civilian life are told in this book.

2. "Let the word go forth from this time and place, to friend

recent example would be the terrorist attacks on September 11, 2001, which some people have cited as their reason for enlisting.

War stories are not only about combat; the process of coming home is also part of veterans' stories, and these experiences reflect the individual situation each veteran faced. What kind of welcome home did the veteran experience, if any? How does a veteran reconcile what he or she has experienced in war with the beliefs and value system he or she lived by in the civilian world? Can he or she incorporate the war experience into his or her life story as a whole in a way that gives it some kind of meaning? These questions can take years to resolve. My experience of coming home from the Vietnam War has never really reached a conclusion; as I have grown older, I have gained new insights into the historical context as well as my own motivations and reactions. And for those who come home with a permanent injury or disability, how they coped with the aftereffects of war is a lifelong story.

I personally find "coming home" stories to be more interesting than battle narratives. These are not just war stories; they are human stories. They are about facing and overcoming post-service challenges, about coping with an environment that may or may not have been sympathetic, about courage shown long after the battlefield.

---

and foe alike, that the torch has been passed to a new generation of Americans—born in this century, tempered by war, disciplined by a hard and bitter peace, proud of our ancient heritage—and unwilling to witness or permit the slow undoing of those human rights to which this nation has always been committed, and to which we are committed today at home and around the world. And so, my fellow Americans: ask not what your country can do for you—ask what you can do for your country." "President John F. Kennedy's Inaugural Address (1961)," lines 19, 20.

Despite the uniqueness of every veteran's experience, there is a common theme that I have observed among the veterans I have known. Many veterans feel a deep connection to other vets. There is something about going through training and living within the military that gives us an understanding of each other that needs no words.

I have seen this connection at work in groups of veterans despite differences in our military experience. There may be some good-natured rivalry among the different branches of the service, but this is overshadowed by a feeling of brotherhood and sisterhood. Veterans often share funny stories about things we did, or things the military did that we thought were idiotic.

This sense of connection may be part of the reason some veterans join together in veterans organizations later in life. There is more to it than the acceptance and camaraderie that these organizations offer; together, veterans find ways to help their brother and sister veterans. Organizations may do such things as engaging in advocacy, providing information about places to get help, maintaining local veterans memorials, keeping veterans in the public eye by participating in parades and civic events, providing an honor guard at funerals, and even doing acts of kindness as simple as providing fruit baskets for vets returning home after a stay in the hospital.

I believe the sense of camaraderie and commitment to each other that I have felt had its roots in my time in the service. As soon as I arrived at Fort Dix as a new recruit, I found myself needing to bond with other recruits as we adjusted to what seemed a frightening new life. Besides this natural reaction to an unfamiliar and stressful situation, I found that the Army encouraged our working together. We succeeded or failed as a team.

In combat situations, I was aware of a strong ethic within the military that we take care of each other. We do not abandon wounded comrades on the battlefield. We do not leave our dead behind. It was a sacred commitment that we did not even question.

As a still inexperienced medic with an infantry unit in Vietnam, I witnessed a lieutenant risk his life to retrieve the body of one of our men after an unsuccessful attempt to capture a hill from a company of North Vietnamese Army soldiers.

> The firing had stopped, except for an occasional round that shot by over our heads with an eerie whizzing sound. Some of the grass was in flames. Rucksacks and equipment were scattered everywhere. "Lieutenant Repp took an NVA bunker," someone was saying. "Killed three NVA with hand grenades and captured an AK-47." "We're moving back down," Sergeant Carter was yelling. But first Lieutenant Repp would go back up to recover the body. He moved up the hill, followed by the machine gunner and ammo bearer, and disappeared over the crest toward the NVA positions. Minutes went by as I watched the crest. Suddenly Lieutenant Repp ran back down the hill dragging a body . . .[3]

Joe DeFazio's book reminds me of this ideal of loyalty among soldiers. He does more than share his experiences as a veteran; he uses what he has learned to help other vets. His effort to provide information and encouragement to other vets struggling with service-related disabilities exemplifies a saying that I think would resonate with the vets I know: "Leave no veteran behind."

---

3. McDaniel, *Walk Through the Valley*, 87–88.

Joe is in an excellent position to help veterans dealing with disabilities and the process of seeking benefits because he has himself struggled with those problems.

The Bible sheds light on how our experiences of suffering can equip us to help others. In his second letter to the Christians in Corinth, the apostle Paul praises God for comforting him in his affliction so that he may be able to comfort others.[4] The sufferings or problems a person endures may make that person uniquely equipped to help other people facing the same problem. In this way, God turns our sufferings into a means for comforting and encouraging others.

Common experience confirms this truth. Someone who has dealt with a problem is best able to understand and empathize with others facing it. This gives him credibility. Concern that arises from a shared experience of suffering can go beyond words and reach into the heart. It can establish a bond that creates room for healing.

A person who has actually faced a problem in his or her own life may have developed practical methods of coping that may be helpful to others. He may be able to warn of unexpected problems that may pop up and know how to prepare for them. She may have discovered resources that can help. In all these ways, he is equipped to help others.

---

4. "Praise be to the God and Father of our Lord Jesus Christ, the Father of compassion and the God of all comfort, who comforts us in all our troubles, so that we can comfort those in any trouble with the comfort we ourselves receive from God. For just as we share abundantly in the sufferings of Christ, so also our comfort abounds through Christ. If we are distressed, it is for your comfort and salvation; if we are comforted, it is for your comfort, which produces in you patient endurance of the same sufferings we suffer. And our hope for you is firm, because we know that just as you share in our sufferings, so also you share in our comfort." 2 Cor 1:3–7, NIV.

Joe mentions the benefits of getting out and being with other people. This has certainly been an important part of my "coming home" as a veteran.

In the years immediately after I left the Army, two groups of friends were very important to me. One was a five-member "Jesus rock" band that played at festivals and coffeehouses during the Jesus People movement of the early 1970s. A few years later, I was part of a group of four who met in an apartment for Bible study and prayer. In later years, wherever I was, I would find welcome and friendship in a church.

After the South Vietnamese government fell, I met Vietnamese refugees who remain my friends to this day. After several years, I realized my need to connect with fellow vets and I found friends in Vietnam Veterans of America. My parents and two brothers had been supportive; by my mid-thirties I had a wife and family of my own.

These relationships have helped define my post-Army life. They reflect the fact that the Vietnam War will always be part of me, but it is not my whole life.

Joe also encourages veterans to have faith. I would like to add some words about my own experience.

I had come to faith in Christ at the age of fourteen and that influenced how I saw the world of the late 1960s and my place in it. When the Vietnam War escalated and pulled in more and more young men my age, I came to a belief that serving in Vietnam was what I was supposed to do. As the war became controversial, my own sense of what I should do was clarified: I would enlist for the medics. How could I have navigated that difficult time in my own life and that of our country if I did not have some structure of belief and values?

Probably the most important factor in my coming out of the Vietnam War reasonably intact is that my job in the war fit my temperament and values. This is not to suggest that the way was always clear to me, or that I found my job in Vietnam easy. Not at all! One year in the war was my limit. It took everything I had to get through that year, and many years afterward to put it all into perspective. But I believed in what I was doing.

In Vietnam I had seen what human beings are capable of in war: violence, killing, fighting for survival. It was a different world from anything I had experienced in civilian life, a different way of being human, and therefore a different potential within myself. Because of my faith, I did not lose my bearings or my sense of what I was supposed to do. My faith gave me a broader perspective than the war I was experiencing day to day, a vision of something better. What I saw in the war would not define who I was.

In the years immediately after my discharge, faith kept me from despair or unfocused anger as I became disillusioned about the war and cynical about the political leadership that had kept us in it. Faith made me better able to recognize and accept the sadness I felt over what I saw in the war, as that emotion emerged years later.

Since I came home from Vietnam, faith has given me a broader perspective than the difficult experiences in my own life. The world, and my life, are much larger than whatever problem or pain or grief I am dealing with right now. This faith has helped me to keep going, to do what I have to do, in the expectation that good will eventually come of it, or at least as much good as is possible in this world.

When I was in Vietnam, I remembered the verse in the Bible in which Jesus invites those of us who "labor and are heavy laden" to come to him for rest, to share his yoke and learn from him, and to "find rest for your souls."[5]

---

5. "Come to me, all you who are weary and burdened, and I will give you rest. Take my yoke upon you and learn from me, for I am

> Jesus offers rest, and he offers a yoke. A yoke is meant for two. Jesus is not handing us a burden, but inviting us to bear the same burden he is bearing, along with him. It is his yoke and he shares it with us . . .[6]

That compassionate invitation still gives me hope.

I appreciate this opportunity to add some words to Joe's book. Joe, I salute you for sharing your story and insights with us. I hope your book will provide information and inspiration for many of our brother and sister veterans.

Leave no veteran behind!

---

gentle and humble in heart." Matt 11:28–30, NIV.
6. McDaniel, *Walk Through the Valley*, 131.

About the Authors

Julia Davis holds an EdM from the Harvard Graduate School of Education and an EdM from Bouve College of Human Development at Northeastern University. She has held teaching certificates in New York, Massachusetts, and the District of Columbia and has been certified as an Assistant Principal and as an Assistant Special Education Supervisor. Julia has taught in the public and private sector in community-based programs including METCO, summer STEP opportunities for underrepresented populations in science and technology, and Head Start. She has served as a member of Parent's Advocacy Group for Massachusetts, supporting FAPE and mainstreaming special education students. She has taught pre-K through twelfth grade and courses for adult non-readers, limited English language learners, and GED preparation. Julia taught internationally as an undergraduate exchange student in a special education program based in Newnham on Severn, Gloucestershire, England, which operated under the auspices of Antioch College in Ohio. Julia and her husband, Dan, have three children and three grandchildren. They attend the International Family Church in North Reading, Massachusetts. Julia developed a monthly prayer breakfast program for the Everett, Massachusetts community.[1]

Jeanne DeFazio is a SAG/AFTRA actress of Spanish/Italian descent who played supporting parts in theater, movies, and television series and then disappeared into a life of service to the marginalized in the drama of real life. Jeanne became a teacher of second-language-learner children in the barrios of San Diego. A woman of great faith, intelligence, and energy, she completed a Bachelor of Arts in history at the University of California, Davis, pursued seminary education at Gordon-Conwell Theological Seminary (MAR theology), and completed the Cal State TEACH English language learners program. In 2009 to the present, Jeanne has returned as an Athanasian Teaching Scholar at Gordon Conwell's multicultural Boston Center for Urban Ministerial Education (CUME), which serves the often unnoticed but thriving ethnic churches.[2] Email Jeanne at jcdefazio55@gmail.com.

John Joseph (Joe) DeFazio served his country in the U.S. Army as a Specialist Fourth Class and as an administrator at the United States Department of the Interior. He is a lifetime member of Disabled American Veterans (DAV), a member of the American Legion, and has participated in fundraiser events for the Wounded Warrior Project. Joe loves fishing, shooting, gardening, cooking, and reading American history. He resides in Davis, California. Email Joe at jjdefazio@gmail.com.

1. DeFazio and Spencer, *Empowering English Language Learners*, 150–51.

2. Flowers and DeFazio, *How to Have an Attitude of Gratitude*, viii–ix.

About the Authors

Bruce I. McDaniel enlisted in the Army in September 1967 and remained on active duty until January 1971. He trained for the MOS (Military Occupational Specialty) 91A (Medical Care and Treatment) at Fort Sam Houston, Texas and spent a year as a medic with the 1st Battalion, 52nd Infantry, 198th Infantry Brigade in Vietnam. Subsequent military assignments took him to Fort Benning, Georgia; Fort Sam Houston, Texas; and Fort Bragg, North Carolina. Bruce is a life member of Vietnam Veterans of America and served as editor of two of Chapter 20's publications. He self-published a book about his Vietnam War experiences and a collection of short stories on the theme of coming home from the war. Recently retired from a career in legal writing and indexing, Bruce lives in Rochester, New York with his wife, Thurma. He is active in a Methodist church.

Martha Reyes was born in Puerto Rico and has resided in California, ministering to Hispanics in the United States and internationally since 1978. She has traveled to more than twenty-two Latin American countries and many parts of Europe and the Middle East, giving concerts and retreats on inner healing and participating as a guest speaker in national and international conventions on healing and restoration. From 1992 until the year 2000 she organized the acclaimed Hosanna Multi-Festivals conventions, international events with representatives from thirty countries in music, theater, and arts, held annually in Mexico, Florida, and Israel.[3]

---

3. DeFazio and Spencer, *Redeeming the Screens*, 90–91.

Bibliography

Arnold, Jonathan. "Racial Differences in Veteran Service Connection Disability." St. Catherine University Master of Social Work Clinical Research Papers. May 2017. https://sophia.stkate.edu/cgi/viewcontent.cgi?article=1705&context=msw_papers.

DeFazio, Jeanne, and John P. Lathrop, eds. *Creative Ways to Build Christian Community*. House of Prisca & Aquila Series. Eugene, OR: Wipf & Stock, 2013.

DeFazio, Jeanne, and William David Spencer, eds. *Empowering English Language Learners: Successful Strategies of Christian Educators*. House of Prisca & Aquila Series. Eugene, OR: Wipf & Stock, 2018.

———, eds. *Redeeming the Screens: Living Stories of Media "Ministers" Bringing the Message of Jesus Christ to the Entertainment Industry*. House of Prisca & Aquila Series. Eugene, OR: Wipf & Stock, 2016.

Flowers, Teresa, and Jeanne DeFazio. *How to Have an Attitude of Gratitude on the Night Shift*. Eugene, OR: Resource, 2014.

Got Questions Ministries. "Is the war in heaven in Revelation 12 describing Satan's original fall or an end time's angelic battle?" https://www.gotquestions.org/war-in-heaven.html.

"Governor Jackson Sign Bill to Help Veterans and Protect Public Safety." August 7, 2017. https://sd19.senate.ca.gov/news/2017-08-07-governor-signs-jackson-bill-help-veterans-and-protect-public-safety.

BIBLIOGRAPHY

Harris Federal Employee Law Firm. "Veterans' Affairs (VA) Disability Benefits." https://www.federaldisability.com/legal-services/va-disability/.

"Homeless Veterans in the United States." Revolvy. https://www.revolvy.com/page/Homeless-veterans-in-the-United-States.

Lincott, Anne. "PTSD and Vietnam Veterans: Part Two: Substance Abuse." *Hill and Ponton* (blog), May 20, 2016. https://www.hillandponton.com/ptsd-vietnam-veterans-part-2-substance-abuse/.

MacNeill, Arianna. "Group, city eyes upgrades at Independence Park." *Salem News*, January 5, 2017. https://www.salemnews.com/news/local_news/group-city-eyes-upgrades-at-independence-park/article_adc4af25-fd92-5d78-a66f-30f5a161388a.html.

McDaniel, Bruce I. *Walk Through the Valley: The Spiritual Journey of a Vietnam War Medic*. Raleigh, NC: Lulu, 2016.

National Coalition for Homeless Veterans. "Background & Statistics." http://nchv.org/index.php/news/media/background_and_statistics/.

"President John F. Kennedy's Inaugural Address (1961)." *Our Documents: 100 Milestone Documents from the National Archives*. https://www.ourdocuments.gov/doc.php?flash=false&doc=91.

Puntillo, Ted. "How to Disagree with a Veterans Administration Decision." Military Connection. https://militaryconnection.com/veterans-scene/how-to-disagree-with-a-veterans-administration-decision/.

———. "New veteran's treatment seeks 'battle buddy' mentors." *The Reporter*, November 22, 2014, |updated August 29, 2018. https://www.thereporter.com/2014/11/22/guest-new-veterans-treatment-seeks-battle-buddy-mentors/.

"Puntillo honored as Veteran of the Year." *Davis Enterprise*, June 30, 2012. https://www.davisenterprise.com/local-news/state-government/puntillo-honored-as-veteran-of-the-year/.

Robbins, Katherine Gallagher, and Anusha Ravi. "Veterans Living Paycheck to Paycheck Are under Threat During Budget Debates." Center for American Progress, September 19, 2017. https://www.americanprogress.org/issues/poverty/news/2017/09/19/439023/veterans-living-paycheck-paycheck-threat-budget-debates/.

Sharma, Amita. "The only city in California to solve veteran homelessness is on a mission to go bigger." *CalMatters*, May 18, 2018. https://calmatters.org/articles/the-only-city-in-california-to-solve-veteran-homelessness-is-on-a-mission-to-go-bigger/.

Bibliography

United States Bureau of Labor Statistics. "43.3 percent of veterans with a service-connected disability were employed in August 2015." *TED: The Economics Daily*, November 10, 2016. https://www.bls.gov/opub/ted/2016/43-point-3-percent-of-veterans-with-a-service-connected-disability-were-employed-in-august-2015.htm.

United States Census Bureau. "Veterans Day 2017: Nov. 11." October 12, 2017. https://www.census.gov/newsroom/facts-for-features/2017/veterans-day.html.

United States Department of Housing and Urban Development. "2018 Annual Homeless Assessment Report to Congress." December 2018. https://files.hudexchange.info/resources/documents/2018-AHAR-Part-1.pdf .

United States Veterans Affairs. "Veteran Poverty Trends." May 2015. https://www.va.gov/vetdata/docs/SpecialReports/Veteran_Poverty_Trends.pdf.

United States War Dogs Association. "Vietnam Statistics." http://www.uswardogs.org/vietnam-statistics/.

Wounded Warrior Project. "Mission Statement." https://www.woundedwarriorproject.org/mission.

Ward, Bob. "A Homeless Vet Living in the Shadows." Boston 25 News, February 13, 2019. https://www.boston25news.com/news/a-homeless-vet-living-in-the-shadows/914655659

Wikipedia. "DD Form 214." https://en.wikipedia.org/wiki/DD_Form_214.

———. "Farmer Veteran Coalition." https://en.m.wikipedia.org/wiki/Farmer_Veteran_Coalition.

www.ingramcontent.com/pod-product-compliance
Lightning Source LLC
Chambersburg PA
CBHW071313060426
42444CB00034B/2483